Tajweed Made Easy

Compiled by Khalid Idris

© 2016 Khalid Idris

All rights reserved. No part of this book can be reproduced, transmitted or stored in any form or by any means, electronic or otherwise including internet, photocopying, recording, or any other storage and retrieval system without written permission of the publisher.

ISBN: 978-1-326-74623-0

Contents and Checklist

Introduction
About the Compiler
Chain of Authority (sanad) in Qur'an
The Importance of Tajweed
Intro Lesson: The Major and Minor Mistakes ☐
Part 1: Pronouncing the Letters Correctly
Lesson 1: The Empty Space in the Mouth ☐
Lesson 2: The Throat ☐
Lesson 3: The Tongue (Part 1) ☐
Lesson 4: The Tongue (Part 2) ☐
Lesson 5: The Tongue (Part 3) ☐
Lesson 6: The Tongue (Part 4) ☐
Lesson 7: The Tongue (Part 5) ☐
Lesson 8: The Tongue (Part 6) ☐
Lesson 9: The Tongue (Part 7) ☐
Lesson 10: The Lips ☐
Lesson 11: The Nose ☐
Lesson 12: The Permanent Qualities (Sifaat) which have Opposites (Part 1) ☐
Lesson 13: The Permanent Qualities of Letters which have Opposites (Part 2) ☐
Lesson 14: The Permanent Qualities of Letters which have Opposites (Part 3) ☐
Lesson 15: The Permanent Qualities of Letters which have Opposites (Part 4) ☐

Lesson 16: The Permanent Qualities of Letters which have Opposites (Part 5) ☐
Lesson 17: Permanent Qualities without Opposites (Part 1) ☐
Lesson 18: Permanent Qualities without Opposites (Part 2) ☐
Lesson 19: Permanent Qualities without Opposites (Part 3) ☐
Lesson 20: The *Laam* of Allah ☐
Lesson 21: The Rules of the Letter *Raw* (Part 1) ☐
Lesson 22: The Rules of the Letter *Raw* (Part 2) ☐

Part 2: The Rules of *Noon Saakin* and *Meem Saakin*
Lesson 23: *Izhaar* ☐
Lesson 24: *Idghaam* with *Ghunnah* ☐
Lesson 25: *Idghaam* without *Ghunnah* ☐
Lesson 26: *Qalb* ☐
Lesson 27: *Ikhfaa* (Light *Ghunnah*) ☐
Lesson 28: *Meem Saakin* (Part 1) ☐
Lesson 29: *Meem Saakin* (Part 2) ☐

Part 3: The Rules of *Madd*
Lesson 30: *Madd* (Part 1) ☐
Lesson 31: *Madd* (Part 2) ☐

Part 4: The Rules of Stopping and Continuing Recitation
Lesson 32: The Rules of *Waqf* (Stopping) ☐

Lesson 33: *Alif* and Stopping ☐
Lesson 34: The Stopping and Continuing Symbols ☐

Part 5: Additional Important Matters
Lesson 35: The Amount Symbols ☐
Lesson 36: The 14 *Sajdah Ayats* ☐

My Personal Advice and Tips for Teachers
Bibliography

Introduction

All praise belongs to Allah; blessings be upon His slave and final messenger, Muhammad and on his family, his companions and all those who follow the guidance which came through him.

The idea for writing a Tajweed textbook which was organised and simple for English-speaking students occurred in a meeting at my local madrasah. I was given the task to compile it. Whilst teaching, I would edit the textbook, so that it would be easy for students to understand and apply the rules of Tajweed.

The Qur'an is the word of Allah. Hence, its recitation must be taken seriously. The purpose of the science of Tajweed is to make the reader recite the Qur'an correctly the way it was intended. Through this science the person can recite the Qur'an according to the way of the Prophet Muhammad (peace be upon him) who received it from the angel Jibra'eel who received it from Allah The Most High.

If you are completely new to Tajweed then I would recommend studying under a person who has already studied the subject in detail. This book could be used as an organised course, where you, the learner, will know your progress as you tick the boxes and put a date next to them.

Alternatively, you could listen to recordings of Shaykhs who are known for their Tajweed and copy the way they pronounce and use the rules of Tajweed which are mentioned in this book. The downfall in this method is that some who copy recordings, only copy the tune of the Shaykh and not the Tajweed. This is because they do not have a 'trained ear' to pick up on their own mistakes. So in a nutshell, a Tajweed teacher is highly recommended, and only as a last resort, accurately copy recordings of Shaykhs known for their Tajweed.

I would like to express my sincerest gratitude to my teachers, colleagues and my thanks to all who advised me to publish this book. May Allah accept this humble effort, forgive our mistakes and help us with the correct recitation of His Book which pleases Him.

Khalid Idris
Dewsbury
24/08/16

Feel free to ask any questions:
Email: khalid.midris@hotmail.com

About the Compiler

Khalid was born and brought up in West Yorkshire, England. During his secondary school, he enrolled in The Institute of Islamic Education in Dewsbury, UK. He spent eight years full-time studying the higher Islamic sciences at the institute. It was here that he began his journey of learning Tajweed and having a passion for it. In 2009, he graduated with a BA in Islamic Sciences and Arabic Literature. In 2016, he graduated from The Open University with an Upper Second-class BA Honours in English Language and Literature.

As head of the Tajweed department at a local madrasah in Dewsbury for several years, he had the opportunity to create a syllabus and targets for all the classes taught there. He currently teaches Tajweed and has taught the Jamiat Ulama syllabus in Fiqh, Aqaaid, Taareekh and Aadaab, levels 1, 2, 3, 4, and 5 to children aged from 7-12. He also teaches children and adults privately on weekends, online as well as locally.

Chain of Authority (sanad) in Qur'an

The compiler of this book (Khalid ibn Idris), learnt the Holy Qur'an in the riwayat of Imam Hafs (rahimahullah) and studied the following books of Tajweed: At-Tajweed, Jamalul Qur'an, Muqaddimah Al-Jazariyyah, Jamiul Waqf, Khulastul Bayan from: Shaykh Imtiaz Ahmad Wali who read by Shaykh Fadlur Rahman Azami, who read by Shaykh Mustafa al Azami, who read by Shaykh Riyasat Ali, who read by Qari Ziya Al-Deen (d. 1952 C.E.), who read by Qari Abdur Rahman Al-Makki (d. 1923 C.E.), who read by Qari Abdullah ibn Basheer Al-Makki (d. 1919 C.E.), who read by Ibrahim Sa'd (d. 1898 C.E.), who read by Shaykh Hasan Al-Juraysi Al-Kabeer (was still alive in 1888 C.E.), who read by Shaykh Muhammad Al-Mutawalli, who read by Shaykh Ahmad Al-Durri Al-Tihami (died before 1867 C.E.),
who read by Shaykh Ahmad Salamunah (was still alive in 1818 C.E.),
who read by Shaykh Ibraheem Al-Ubaydi (was still alive in 1822 C.E.),
who read by Shaykh Abdur Rahman Al-Ujhuri (d. 1784 C.E.),
who read by Shaykh Ahmad Al-Baqari (d. 1775 C.E.),
who read by Shaykh Muhammad Al-Baqari (d. 1699 C.E.),

who read by Shaykh Abdur Rahman Al-Yemeni (d. 1640 C.E.),

who read by his father Shaykh Shahhadhah Al-Yemeni (d. 1570 C.E.), then from Shaykh Abdul Haq As-Sunbati from the aforementioned Shaykh Shahhadah Al-Yemeni (d. 1570 C.E.),

who read by Shaykh Nasir Al-Deen At-Tablawi (d. 1559 C.E.),

who read by Shaykh al-Islam Zakariyya Al-Ansari (d. 1519 C.E.),

who read by Shaykh Ridwan Al-Uqbi (d. 1448 C.E.),

who read by the auto of An-Nashr Imam Muhammad ibn Al-Jazari (d. 1430 C.E.),

who read by Shaykh Abdur Rahman Al-Baghdadi (d. 1379 C.E.),

who read by Shaykh Muhammad ibn Ahmad As-Sa'igh (d. 1325 C.E.),

who read by the son-in-law of Imam Shatibi Al-Kamal Ali ibn Shuja (d. 1263 C.E.),

who read by Imam Al-Shatibi (d. 1194 C.E.)

who read by Shaykh Ali ibn Hudhayl Al-Balansi,

who read by Shaykh Abu Dawud Sulayman ibn Najah,

who read by Imam Abu Amr Al-Dani,

who read by Shaykh Tahir ibn Ghalbun,

who read by Abu Hasan Al-Hashimi,

who read by Shaykh Abu Abbas Ahmad bin Sahal Al-Ushnani,

who read by Shaykh Ubayd ibn Sabbah,

who read by Imam Hafs ibn Sulayman Al-Asadi,
who read by Imam Asim ibn Abi Al-Najud Al Asadi Al-Kufi,
who read by Imam Abu Abdur Rahman Al-Sulami,
who read by Zaid ibn Thabit, Ubayy ibn K'ab, who read by Ali ibn Abi Talib, Uthman ibn Affan, Abdullah ibn Masood (may Allah be pleased with them all),
who read by the last and final messenger **Muhammad** (sallallahu 'alaihi wa sallam), who read by Jibra-eel ('alaihis salaam), who brought it from Lowhul Mahfooz where it was presented by **Allah** (subhanahu wa ta'aalaa).

The Importance of Tajweed

Imam Ibn Al-Jazari (may Allah have mercy upon him) was a great Qur'an and Hadeeth scholar of the 9th Hijri century. His famous poem about the rules of Tajweed called *Al-Muqaddimah al-Jazariyyah* is taught in higher Islamic education institutes globally. In his poem, the imam writes:

'And applying Tajweed is an issue of absolute necessity,
Whoever doesn't apply Tajweed to the Quran, then a sinner is he.'

It becomes clear why a person is sinful when one studies how delicate the Arabic language is. Take for example, the word *qalb* and *kalb*. *Qalb* (with a *qaaf*) means heart, and *kalb* (with a *kaaf*) means dog in Arabic, by changing the sound of just one letter the meaning has changed significantly. Changes in meaning such as this would also affect one's prayer (salah).

Mistakes in Tajweed are described as *lahn*. There are two types of mistakes: Major (jalee) and minor (khafee).

To recite the Quraan with Major mistakes

intentionally is a major sin which can lead one to disbelief *(kufr)*. To make Minor mistakes is disliked (makrooh), although minor mistakes do not necessarily change the meaning of the Qur'an, they do in fact deprive the Holy Qur'an of its real beauty. Therefore, it is very important to learn the rules of Tajweed.

Examples of the Major Mistakes

1. To pronounce a letter incorrectly (by not reading the letter from its place of sound and with its permanent qualities)

To read الْحَمْدُ as الْهَمْدُ

To read ثُمَّ as سُمَّ

To read طَارِقٌ as تَارِكٌ

To read صَيْفٌ as سَيْفٌ

To read الَّذِيْنَ as الَّزِيْنَ

To read عَلِمَ as أَلَمَ

2. To add a letter (usually the letter *wow*, *yaa* or *alif* is added) (additon)

To read رَبِّ

as رَبِّيْ

To read نَعْبُدُ

as نَعْبُدُوْ

To read أَنْعَمْتَ

as أَنْعَمْتَا

3. To miss a letter out (omission)

To read أَنْزَلْنَا

as أَنْزَلْنَ

To read اَلَّتِيْ

as اَلَّتِ

To read رَسُوْلًا

as رَسُلًا

4. To replace a harkat (zabar, zeyr, peysh) with a sukoon

To read خَلَقَ

as خَلْقَ

To read وَالْقَمَرِ

as وَالْقَمْرِ

To read اِبِلٌ

as اِبْلٌ

To read كَبُرَ

as كَبْرَ

5. To replace a sukoon with a harkat (zabar, zeyr, peysh)

To read أَغْنَى

as أَغَنَى

To read حَجْرٍ

as حَجَرٍ

The Major Mistakes Activity

Write your own examples of Major mistakes. Give two examples for each of the the five types of Major mistakes mentioned above. (15-20 mins)

Examples of the Minor Mistakes

To read an empty mouth letter as a full mouth letter, or a full mouth letter as an empty mouth letter. For example, ط is a full mouth letter, to read it with a flat sound (empty mouth) would be a minor mistake.

Another type of minor mistake is to miss out *Izhar, Idgham, Ikhfa* or *Qalb*. To miss out *Madd* (elongating) is also a minor mistake. These rules will be covered in the book *insha-Allah*.

The Minor Mistakes Activity

(1) Write a list of at least 3 mistakes which are counted as Minor mistakes.

(2) What is the ruling of making minor mistakes:
(a) Prohibited (Haram)
(b) Disliked (Makrooh)
(c) Encouraged (Mustahab)

(5 mins)

PART 1: SAYING THE LETTERS CORRECTLY

Makhraj means the place where the sound of the letter comes from. We will start off with the *makhraj* of each letter and then move onto the *sifaat* (permanent qualities) of the letters. In order to pronounce any letter perfectly, the letter must be pronounced with its *makhraj* (point of articulation) and its *sifaat* (permanent qualities).

Lesson 1 The Empty Space in the Mouth and Throat

The Empty Space in the Mouth and Throat is used for the three vowel sounds of the Arabic language.

The aa sound in ا

The ou sound in اُوْ

The ee sound in اِيْ

Tick the box when you know how to say the vowel sounds. (If you think it's helpful you can even write a date next to the boxes as you complete them):

I know how to say the vowel sounds ☐

<u>Activity 1.1</u>

Without looking in the book, in pairs, tell each other the three vowel sounds and where their sound comes from?
(5 mins)

Lesson 2 The Throat

ء ه (hamzah, haa)
Bottom of the throat is used for these two letters.

ح ع ('ayn, 'haa)
Middle of the throat is used for these two letters.

خ غ (ghayn, khaw)
Top of the throat is used for these two letters.

Tick the boxes when you know how to say these letters:

I know how to say ء ه ☐

I know how to say ح ع ☐

I know how to say خ غ ☐

Activity 1.2
Without looking in the book, in pairs, tell each other where the sound of the letters covered today comes from? (5 mins)

Lesson 3 The Tongue (Part 1)

قْ *(qaaf)*

Back of the tongue touches the **soft palate** above it.

كْ *(kaaf)*

Back of the tongue touches the **hard palate** above it. (The back of the tongue used for the *kaaf* will be a little more forward than the part of the tongue used for the *qaaf*).

Note: The *qaaf* and *kaaf* are close in their sound, but you can tell the difference between them by the soft palate and the hard palate.

Tick the boxes when you know how to say these letters:

I know how to say قْ ☐

I know how to say كْ ☐

Activity 1.3
Without looking in the book, in pairs, tell each other where the sound of the letters covered today comes from? (5 mins)

Lesson 4 The Tongue (Part 2)

Middle part of the tongue touches the hard palate. This is the same for these three letters:

ج ش ى (*jeem, sheen, yaa*)

Note: The *jeem* should be pronounced like you say the 'J' sound in 'jump' (it's a hard sound – we don't say jhump).

Hardly any mistakes are made in these letters as they are found in other languages.

Tick the boxes when you know how to say these letters:

I know how to say ج ☐

I know how to say ش ☐

I know how to say ى ☐

Activity 1.4

Without looking in the book, in pairs, tell each other where the sound of the letters covered today comes from? (5 mins)

Lesson 5 The Tongue (Part 3)

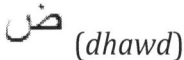 (*dhawd*)

One side of the tongue touches the **upper pre-molars and molars**. (You have a choice as to which part of the tongue is used: Use either the left side of the tongue only (which is most commonly used), or the right side only or both sides of the tongue). (According to one of my teachers, Umar [May Allah be pleased with him] would use both sides of his tongue to pronounce this letter).

Tick the box when you know how to say this letter:

I know how to say ض ☐

Activity 1.5

Without looking in the book, in pairs, tell each other where the sound of the letters covered today comes from? (5 mins)

Lesson 6 The Tongue (Part 4)

ل *(laam)*

Tip of the tongue with any side of the tongue touches the gums of the upper two front teeth (incisors) to the gums of the first premolars.

ن *(noon)*

Tip of the tongue with any side of the tongue touches the gums of the upper two teeth (incisors) to the gums of the canines.

Difference between *laam* and *noon*: in *laam* the area of the gums is until the first premolars, whereas in the *noon* the area of the gums is only until the canines. Again, no one hardly makes mistakes in *laam* and *noon* because they are found in other languages.

ر *(raw)*

Tip of the tongue with a small area of the upper part of the tongue touches the gums behind the upper two teeth (incisors).

Note: *raw* and the letter 'R': In Arabic, the *raw* is pronounced with the tip of the tongue, and the letter 'R' in English is pronounced with the middle of the tongue. For example, in English we say Arabic, in Arabic we say Arabi – a teacher will be able to pronounce them differently.

A mistake some people make is that they repeat *raw* when pronouncing it. Like, *Arrrrrrahmanirrrrraheem*. This must be avoided.

Tick the boxes when you know how to say these letters:

I know how to say ل ☐

I know how to say ت ☐

I know how to say ر ☐

Activity 1.6

Without looking in the book, in pairs, tell each other where the sound of the letters covered today comes from? (5 mins)

Lesson 7 The Tongue (Part 5)

ط د ت *(taw, daal, taa)*

Tip of the tongue touches the gums of the upper two teeth (incisors).

Note: The *daal* is not an English 'D' sound, in Arabic we say Adam, in English we say Adam. A teacher will be able to show the difference in how they are pronounced. For the English 'D,' only the tip of the tongue is used. For *daal*, the tip of the tongue as well as the upper part of the tongue is used.

Tick the boxes when you know how to say these letters:

I know how to say ط ☐
I know how to say د ☐
I know how to say ت ☐

Activity 1.7

1. Without looking in the book, in pairs, tell each other where the sound of the letters covered today comes from?   (5 mins)

2. Revise all the letters covered today. Remember revision is key in *Tajweed*. (10 mins)

Lesson 8 The Tongue (Part 6)

ز س ص *(zaa, seen, sawd)*

Tip of the tongue lightly touches the edge of the top and bottom two teeth (incisors).

Note: The *seen* and the *sawd* have a slightly different sound. This is because the tongue will be kept slightly elevated when the *sawd* is pronounced because it is a full mouth letter. For the *seen*, the tongue will be kept flat.

Tick the boxes when you know how to say these letters:

I know how to say ز ☐

I know how to say س ☐

I know how to say ص ☐

Activity 1.8

1. Without looking in the book, in pairs, tell each other where the sound of the letters covered today comes from?   (5 mins)

2. What is the difference between the letter *seen* and letter *sawd*? (3 mins)

Lesson 9 The Tongue (Part 7)

ظ ذ ث *(zhaw, zhaal, thaa)*

Tip of the tongue touches the edge of the upper two teeth (incisors).

Note: The difference between the *zaa* and *zhaal* is that the tongue will be slightly out when pronouncing *zhaal*, and tongue will be in when reading the *zaa*. For *zhaw*, the tongue will be elevated because it is a full mouth letter, whilst touching the edge of the upper two teeth. *Zhaal* and *zaa* are both empty mouth letters.

Tick the boxes when you know how to say these letters:

I know how to say ظ ☐

I know how to say ذ ☐

I know how to say ث ☐

Activity 1.9

1. Without looking in the book, in pairs, tell each other where the sound of the letters covered today comes from? (5 mins)

2. What is the difference between the letter *zaa* and letter *zhal*? (3 mins)

3. What is the main difference between letter *zhaw* and letter *zhal*? (3 mins)

Lesson 10 The Lips

Three letters are sounded by using **both lips**.

بـ *(baa)*

Join the wet part of the lips together.

م *(meem)*

Join dry part of the lips together.

و *(wow)*

Join the lips without making the two lips touch.

فـ *(faa)*

The edge of the upper two teeth (incisors) touch the inner part of the bottom lip.

Tick the boxes when you know how to say these letters:

I know how to say بـ ☐

I know how to say م ☐

I know how to say و ☐

I know how to say فـ ☐

Activity 1.10

1. Without looking in the book, in pairs, tell each other where the sound of the letters covered today comes from? (5 mins)

Lesson 11 The Nose

The *ghunnah* sound comes from **the nose**.

$$\text{اِنَّ مِنْ حَبْلٌ مِنْ نِعْمَةٍ مِنْ تُرَاباً كُنْتُ}$$

It sounds like a humming N or M sound.

Tick the box when you know how to do *ghunnah*:

I know how to do *ghunnah* ☐

نْ or نْ

The above are *noon saakins*. If you have an Arabian print Qur'an, the *jazam (sukoon)* will look like the first one (a small full circle), and if you have a South Asian or South African print Qur'an, then the *jazam (sukoon)* will look like the second one (a small broken half circle).

ٌ   ٍ   ً

The above three are called **tanween** in Tajweed. From the left, in Urdu they are called '*do pesh, do zer, do zabar.*' In Arabic they are called '*Dhammatain, kasratain, fathatayn.*'

ِ   ُ   َ

The above three, from the left, in Urdu: *zer*, *pesh* and *zabar*, in Arabic: *kasrah*, *dhammah* and *fathah*. They are also referred to as *harakah* or *harakaat* (plural).

Activity 1.11

1. Without looking in the book, in pairs, tell each other where the sound of the letters covered today comes from?   (5 mins)

Well done! You have covered all the letters, masha-Allah.

2. Revise all the letters because without revision all effort is wasted.

Lesson 12 The Permanent Qualities (Sifaat) which have Opposites (Part 1)

The Permanent Qualities (*Sifaate Laazimah*) are the qualities which are part of the makeup of the letter and cannot be removed from it.

HAMS: When any letter from the following letters has a *jazam (sukoon)* on top of it, the letter will be pronounced whilst the breath continues. This quality is called **Hams** and is found in these letters:

فَحَثَّهُ شَخْصٌ سَكَتْ

So the letters above will have a strong whispering sound (*Hams*) when they have *jazam*, and when they have a *harakah* (*zabar, zeyr, peysh*) they will have a natural *Hums*.

The *kaaf* and *taa* have *Hams* only when they have *jazam*, because they have the quality of *shiddah* also (which will be covered in the next lesson). When pronouncing the letter *seen*, the breath will continue no matter what *harakah* it has.

JAHR: All letters besides *faa, 'haa, thaa, haa, sheen, khaw, sawd, seen, kaaf* and *taa* have the quality called **Jahr** (stopping the airflow). This means when they have a *jazam* on top of them the breath will not
continue when they are pronounced. E.g. أَجْ

Note: To practice the letters with their *sifaat*, add a *hamzah* before the letter and a *jazam* (sukoon) on the letter. E.g. أَفْ

I know how to do *Hams* and *Jahr* ☐

Activity 1.12

1. Have a look in the Holy Qur'aan and find at least three examples of *Hams* and *Jahr*? (10 mins)

(Tip: Remember when the letters have *sukoon/jazam* they will have *hams*).

Lesson 13 The Permanent Qualities of Letters which have Opposites (Part 2)

SHIDDAH: When any letter from the following letters has a *jazam* on top of it, the letter will be pronounced with the sound discontinued. This quality is called **Shiddah**.

اَجِدُ قَطٍّ بَكَتْ

So the sound of these letters will stop in their *makhraj* (place of sound) because they have a hard sound.

RIKHWAH: All letters besides the above-mentioned letters will have their sound continued when they have a *jazam* on top of them. This quality is called **Rikhwah**.

Note: *Hams* in the continuation of breath whereas *Rikhwah* is the continuation of sound.

TAWASSUT: When the following letters have a *jazam* on top of them, the sound will be partially continued and partially discontinued. This quality is called **Tawassut**, and is between *Shiddah* and *Rikhwah*.

لِنْ عُمَرْ

I know how to do *Shiddah*, *Rikhwah* and *Tawassut* ☐

Activity 1.13

1. Have a look in the Holy Qur'aan and find at least three examples of *shiddah* and *tawassut* and *rikhwah*? (15 mins)

Lesson 14 The Permanent Qualities of Letters which have Opposites (Part 3)

IST'ILAA: To elevate the tongue towards the roof of the mouth when pronouncing the letter. This quality is called **Ist'ilaa** (also known as **Tafkheem**) and is found in the following letters:

خُصَّ ضَغْطٍ قِظْ

1st Note: These letters are also called the Full-Mouth Letters because they are pronounced with an upward sound, students find this easier to remember.

2nd Note: In *Ist'ilaa* the focus is that the tongue is raised, whereas in *Itbaaq* the focus is that the tongue makes contact with the hard palate (see the next lesson).

ISTIFAAL: Besides the letter *laam*, the letter *raw* (we will talk about these two later) and the Full-Mouth Letters, the remaining letters are the Empty-Mouth Letters, this is because they are read with a downward sound (also known as a flat sound).

ا ب ت ث ج ح د ذ ز س ش ع ف ك م ن و ي ه

This downward sound quality is called **Istifaal**, where the tongue is kept lowered from the roof of the mouth.

I know how to do *Ist'ilaa* and *Istifaal* ☐

Activity 1.14
1. Have a look in the Holy Qur'aan and find at least three examples of *Ist'ilaa* and *Istifaal*? (10 mins)

Lesson 15 The Permanent Qualities of Letters which have Opposites (Part 4)

ITBAAQ: To press the tongue against the hard palate (roof of the mouth). This quality is called **Itbaaq** and is found in the following four letters:

ص ض ط ظ

The mouth is kept nearly closed when pronouncing the above-mentioned letters.

INFITAAH: The rest of the letters have the quality **Infitaah**, which means that the tongue is kept separated from the mouth when the letter is pronounced. The mouth is kept open when pronouncing these letters. E.g. *baa, taa, thaa, jeem* etc.

I know how to do *Itbaaq* and *Infitaah* ☐

Activity 1.15
1. Have a look in the Holy Qur'aan and find at least three examples of *Itbaaq* and *Infitaah*? (10 mins)

Lesson 16 The Permanent Qualities of Letters which have Opposites (Part 5)

IDHLAAQ: To pronounce the letter with extreme ease from the side of the tongue or lips as if they are slipping away. The quality is called ***Idhlaaq*** and is found in the following letters:

The smooth pronunciation of the above-mentioned letters is due to their places of sound (*makhraj*).

ISMAAT: The rest of the letters will be pronounced with extreme strength coming from their *makhraj*, without which it will not be possible to pronounce the letter. This quality is called ***Ismaat***. Effort is required to pronounce these letters, e.g. *taa, thaa, jeem* etc.

I know how to do *Idhlaaq* and *Ismaat* ☐

Activity 1.16
1. Have a look in the Holy Qur'aan and find at least three examples of *Idhlaaq* and *Ismaat*? (10 mins)

Lesson 17 Permanent Qualities without Opposites (Part 1)

QALQALAH: When any one of these five letters ق ط ب ج د has a *sukoon* on it, there will be a kind of echo sound.

Note: You should be careful not to over-do the echo sound, because it will then sound like you are reading a *zabar (fathah)*.

Three kinds of *Qalqalah*:

Rule 1: If the *Qalqalah* letter has a *sukoon* and is **not** at the end of a word then the echo sound will not be so apparent. Examples:

خَلَقْنٰكُمْ   لَاتَجْزِىٰ   وَجْهَ   قَبْلُ   أَجْرٍ

Rule 2: If the *Qalqalah* letter has a *sukoon* and is at the end of a word which is at the end of a verse then the echo sound will be made apparent.

هَادٍ ۘ   خَلَقَ ۘ   كَسَبَ ۘ   مُحِيطٌ ۘ

Rule 3: If the *Qalqalah* letter has a *tashdeed* on it, then whenever you stop on that letter, the echo sound will slightly continue.

Tick the box when you know how to do the different *Qalqalahs*:

I know how to do *Qalqalah* ☐

Activity 1.17

1. Have a look in the Holy Qur'aan and write at least five examples of *Qalqalah*? (10 mins)

Lesson 18 Permanent Qualities without Opposites (Part 2)

SAFEER: A natural whistle like sound which occurs when pronouncing the letter. This quality is called *Safeer* and is found in the following three letters:

ز س ص

(Note: This whistle sound can even be heard when one is whispering these letters, try it!)

LEEN: When pronouncing the letter, a natural softness and ease found in the letter, where you do not need to force the sound out. This is called *Leen* and is found in *wow saakin* and *yaa saakin* when they come after *zabar (fathah)*. For example, look at the word *khawf* and *sayf* in Arabic.

I know how to do *Safeer* and *Leen* ☐

Activity 1.18
1. Have a look in the Holy Qur'aan and write at least three examples of *Safeer* and *Leen*? (10 mins)

Lesson 19 Permanent Qualities without Opposites (Part 3)

INHIRAAF: The tongue slightly deviates towards the *makhraj* of *raw* while pronouncing the *laam* and vice versa. This quality is called **Inhiraaf** and is found in letter *laam* and letter *raw*.

TAKREER: Rolling the tongue when pronouncing the letter *raw,* which results in the letter *raw* being recited more than once. This quality is called **Takreer** and **must** be avoided.

TAFASSHY: The sound of the letter sheen spreading around the mouth, this is called **Tafasshy** and only found in *sheen*. وَالشَّمْسِ

ISTITAWLAH: The sound of the letter *dhawd* being prolonged throughout its *makhraj*. This quality is called **Istitawlah** and refers to the length of the *makhraj* and is only found in the letter *dhawd*. Especially when it has a *sukoon* on it: فَضْلٍ
وَاخْفِضْ   تَضْلِيْلٍ

I know the qualities of *Inhiraaf, Takreer, Tafasshy* and *Istitawlah* ☐

Activity 1.19

1. Have a look in the Holy Qur'aan and find at least two examples of *Istitawlah*? (5 mins)

2. Explain what *Takreer* is. (3 mins)

3. Find at least three examples of *Tafasshy* in the Holy Qur'aan? (5 mins)

Lesson 20 The *Laam* of Allah

When there is a *zabar* (*fathah*) or *peysh* (*dhammah*) before the *laam* of Allah, then the *laam* will be pronounced full-mouth. E.g.

عَلَى اللهِ   وَمَا جَعَلَهُ اللهُ   مِنَ اللهِ

When there is a *zeyr* (*kasrah*) before the *laam* of Allah, then the *laam* will be pronounced empty-mouth. E.g.

فِىْ سَبِيْلِ اللهِ   لِلّٰهِ   وَبِااللهِ

The *laams* besides Allah's name will be read empty mouth. E.g.

كُلَّهُ   مَا وَلَّهُمْ

I know when the letter *laam* is full-mouth and empty-mouth ☐

(From now on *zabar* will be referred to as *fathah*, *peysh* as *dhammah*, *zeyr* as *kasrah* and *jazam* as *sukoon*).

Activity 1.20

1. Have a look in the Holy Qur'aan and find at least five examples of when the *laam* of Allah is pronounced full-mouth. Explain why.
(10 mins)

2. Have a look in the Holy Qur'aan and find at least five examples of when the *laam* of Allah is pronounced empty-mouth. Explain why.
(10 mins)

3. TRUE OR FALSE: The laams that are not in the name of Allah will also be pronounced with a full-mouth.

Lesson 21 The Rules of the letter *Raw* (Part 1)

If the *raw* has *fathah* or *dhammah* then it will be read with a full-mouth. E.g.

لَبَرَزَ   رُسُلٌ   يَغْفِرُ   طَرَفاً   رَبُّكَ

If the *raw* has a *kasrah* then it will be read with an empty-mouth. E.g.

تَجْرِىْ   ظُهُوْرِهِمْ   وَالزُّبُرِ   رِجَالٌ   رِضْوَانٌ

If the *raw saakin* has a *fathah* or *dhammah* before it, then it will be read with a full-mouth.

فَانْصُرْنَا   اَرْسَلْنَا   يَرْفَعُ   عَرْشٌ   مُرْسَلِيْنَ   اَذْكُرْكُمْ

If the *raw saakin* has a *kasrah* before it, then the *raw* will be read with an empty-mouth.

رَبَّنَا اغْفِرْ لَنَا   اَنْذِرْ   فِرْعَوْنَ   أَحْصِرْتُمْ   وَاسْتَغْفِرْ

Activity 1.21

1. Have a look in the Holy Qur'aan and find at least five examples of when the *raw* is pronounced with a full-mouth. Explain why.
(10 mins)

2. Have a look in the Holy Qur'aan and find at least five examples of when the *raw* is pronounced empty-mouth. Explain why.
(10 mins)

3. Have a look in the Holy Qur'aan and find at least two examples of when the *raw saakin* is pronounced empty-mouth and two examples when it is full-mouth. Explain why.
(10 mins).

Lesson 22 The Rules of the Letter *Raw* (Part 2)

If the *raw mushaddad* has a *fathah* or *dhammah*, then it will be read with a full-mouth. E.g.

$$\text{مِنْ رَّبِّهِمْ} \quad \text{وَلَمْ يُصِرُّوْا} \quad \text{لَيْسَ الْبِرَّ} \quad \text{اَلْحُرُّ}$$
$$\text{فَلَنْ يَّضُرَّ}$$

If the *raw mushaddad* has a *kasrah* before it, then it will be read with an empty-mouth. E.g.

$$\text{مِنْ شَرِّ} \quad \text{بِالْحُرِّ} \quad \text{فِى الرِّقَابِ}$$

If the *raw* you stop on has a *yaa saakin* before it, then it will be read with an empty-mouth regardless of what *harakah* is before the *yaa saakin*. E.g.

$$\text{وَالْكِتَابِ الْمُنِيْرِ۞} \quad \text{خَبِيْرٌ۞} \quad \text{قَدِيْرٌ۞}$$
$$\text{خَيْرٌ۞} \quad \text{بَعِيْرٌ۞}$$

If the *raw saakin* has a full mouth letter after it, then even if there is a *kasrah* before the *raw saakin*, it will still be read with a full-mouth. E.g.

$$\text{فِرْقَةٌ} \quad \text{اِرْصَادًا} \quad \text{قِرْطَاسٍ}$$

I know all the rules of *raw* ☐

Activity 1.22

1. Have a look in the Holy Qur'aan and find at least five examples of when the *raw mushaddad* is pronounced with a full-mouth. Explain why.
(10 mins)

2. Have a look in the Holy Qur'aan and find at least five examples of when the *raw mushaddad* is pronounced empty-mouth. Explain why.
(10 mins)

3. TRUE OR FALSE: If *raw saakin* has a full-mouth letter before it, it will be read with a full-mouth.

PART 2: THE RULES OF NOON SAAKIN AND MEEM SAAKIN

Lesson 23 *Izhaar*

Izhaar is to say the *noon saakin* and *tanween* clearly without *ghunnah*. (*Ghunnah* is covered in lesson 11). After *noon saakin* or *tanween* if any letters of *huroofe halqi:* ء ه ع غ ح خ come then there will be an *Izhaar*.

Noon saakin examples:

مَنْ خَافَ   وَانْحَرْ   وَلِاَنْعِمِكُمْ   عَنْهُ

مِنْ اَيِّ

Tanween examples:

اَجْرٌ غَيْرُ   نَارٌ حَامِيَةٌ

ذَرَّةٍ خَيْرًا   غَاسِقٍ اِذَا   سَلْمٌ هِىَ

Note: Whenever the letter *alif* has a *harakah* (*zabar, zeyr, peysh*) it will be called a *hamzah*.

Tick the box when you know how to do *Izhaar*:
I know how to do *Izhaar* ☐

Activity 2.1

1. Have a look in the Holy Qur'aan and find at least five examples of when there is *Izhaar* in *noon saakin*. Explain why.
(10 mins)

2. Have a look in the Holy Qur'aan and find at least five examples of when there is *Izhaar* in *tanween*. Explain why.
(10 mins)

3. TRUE OR FALSE: If any letters of *huroofe halqi* come after *noon saakin* then there will be a *ghunnah*.

Lesson 24 *Idghaam* with *Ghunnah*

Idghaam means to join two letters together. *Idghaam* has two types, *Idghaam* with *ghunnah* and *Idghaam* without *ghunnah*.

***Idghaam* with *ghunnah*:** After *noon saakin* or *tanween* if any letters from ي و م ن come.

***Noon saakin* examples:**

مِنْ نِّعْمَةٍ   مِنْ مَّسَدٍ   مِنْ وَّالٍ   فَمَنْ يَّعْمَلْ

لَنْ يَّقْدِرَ

***Tanween* examples:**

لَهَبٍ وَّتَبَّ   قَرِيْبًا يَّوْمَ   يَوْمَئِذٍ يَّتَذَكَّرُ

قَرِيْبٍ نُّجِبْ   بِحِجَارَةٍ مِّنْ   حَبْلٌ مِّنْ

Tick the box when you know how to do *Idghaam* with *ghunnah*:

I know how to do *Idghaam* with *ghunnah* ☐

In the following words there will be no *ghunnah* and no *Idghaam*, this is because the *yaa* and the *wow* are in the same word. So even though it may seem like there is *ghunnah* according to the *Idghaam* with *ghunnah* rule, there will be no *ghunnah*.

دُنْيَا   بُنْيَانٌ   قِنْوَانٌ   صِنْوَانٌ

Activity 2.2

1. Have a look in the Holy Qur'aan and find at least five examples of when there is *Idghaam* with *ghunnah* in *noon saakin.* Explain why.
(10 mins)

2. Have a look in the Holy Qur'aan and find at least five examples of when there is *Idghaam* with *ghunnah* in *tanween*. Explain why.
(10 mins)

Lesson 25 *Idghaam* without *Ghunnah*

Remember *Idghaam* has two types, *Idghaam* with *ghunnah* and *Idghaam* without *ghunnah*.

After *noon saakin* or *tanween* if the letter ل or ر comes then there will be an *Idghaam* without *ghunnah*.

***Noon saakin* examples:**

عَنْ رَّبِّهِمْ   كَلَّا لَئِنْ لَّمْ   وَلَمْ يَكُنْ لَّهُ
اَنْ رَّاٰهُ

***Tanween* examples:**

لَعِبْرَةً لِّمَنْ   عِيشَةٍ رَّاضِيَةٍ
شَيْطَانٍ رَّجِيْمٍ   وَيْلٌ لِّكُلِّ

Tick the box when you know how to do *Idghaam* without *ghunnah*:

I know how to do *Idghaam* without *ghunnah* ☐

Activity 2.3

1. Have a look in the Holy Qur'aan and find at least five examples of when there is *Idghaam* without *ghunnah* in *noon saakin.* Explain why.
(10 mins)

2. Have a look in the Holy Qur'aan and find at least five examples of when there is *Idghaam* without *ghunnah* in *tanween*. Explain why.
(10 mins)

Lesson 26 *Qalb*

After *noon saakin* or *tanween* if ب comes, then the *noon saakin* or *tanween* will be **changed into** a *meem* and read as a *meem* with *ghunnah*.

Noon saakin **examples:**

مِنْۢ بَعْدِ   مِنْۢ بَيْنِ   اَنْۢبِيَآءَ   يَنْۢبَغِيْ

Tanween **examples:**

كَافِرٌۢ بِهٖ   عَوَانٌۢ بَيْنَ   بَصِيْرٌۢ بِمَا

Note: Like the above-mentioned examples, there is always a small *meem* between *noon saakin* and *baa* (or between *tanween* and *baa*) when *Qalb* happens. So this would be an easy way to remember when *Qalb* is taking place. But be sure not to get mixed up with the *meem* symbol for stopping which comes at the end of a verse.

Tick the box when you know how to do *Qalb*:
I know how to do *Qalb* ☐

Activity 2.4

1. Have a look in the Holy Qur'aan and find at least five examples of *Qalb* in *noon saakin.* Explain why. (10 mins)

2. Have a look in the Holy Qur'aan and find at least five examples of *Qalb* in *tanween*. Explain why. (10 mins)

Lesson 27 *Ikhfaa* (Light *Ghunnah*)

After *noon saakin* or *tanween* if any letter from

ت ث ج د ذ ز س ش ص ض ط ظ ف ق ك

comes then there will be an *Ikhfaa* (light *ghunnah* meaning a light sound from the nose).

Noon saakin **examples:**

مَنْ ثَقُلَتْ   كُنْتُ تُرْباً

اَنْذَرْنٰكُمْ   وَاَنْزَلْنَا

Tanween **examples:**

سَبْعًا شِدَادًا   خَمْسَةٌ سَادِسُهُمْ

بَلْدَةٌ طَيِّبَةٌ   نَارًا تَلَظّٰى

Tick the box when you know how to do *Ikhfaa*:

I know how to do *Ikhfaa* ☐

Activity 2.5

1. Have a look in the Holy Qur'aan and find at least five examples of *Ikhfaa* in *noon saakin.* Explain why. (10 mins)

2. Have a look in the Holy Qur'aan and find at least five examples of *Ikhfaa* in *tanween.* Explain why. (10 mins)

Lesson 28 *Meem Saakin* (Part 1)

مْ or مْ

The above are *meem saakins*. If you have a Saudi Arabian print Qur'an, the *meem saakin* will look like the left one (full circle on top of it), and if you have a South Asian or South African print Qur'an then the *meem saakin* will look like the one on the right (broken half circle on top of it).

There are three rules to remember for *meem saakin*, *Idghaam meem saakin*, *Ikhfaa meem saakin* and *Izhaar meem saakin*.

Idghaam meem saakin: After *meem saakin* if another *meem* comes then there will be an *Idghaam* with a strong *ghunnah*.

رَسُوْلٌ مِّنْ   فَأَمَّا   اَطْعَمَهُمْ مِّنْ

ثُمَّ   مِمَّا   لَمَّا

I know how to do *Idghaam meem saakin* ☐

Activity 2.6

1. Have a look in the Holy Qur'aan and find at least five examples of *Idghaam meem saakin.* Explain why. (10 mins)

Lesson 29 *Meem Saakin* (Part 2)

Ikhfaa meem saakin: After *meem saakin* if ب comes then there will be an *Ikhfaa* (light *ghunnah*).

اَمْ بِهٖ   عَلَيْهِمْ   بِمُصَيْطِرٍ   تَرْمِيْهِمْ   بِحِجَارَةٍ

وَمَا هُمْ بِمُؤْمِنِيْنَ   اٰتَيْنٰكُمْ بِقُوَّةٍ   هُمْ بِالْاٰخِرَةِ

Izhaar meem saakin: After *meem saakin* if *meem* or *baa* does not come then there will be an *Izhaar* (no *ghunnah*).

رَبِّهِمْ جَنّٰتٍ   وَلَهُمْ عَذَابٌ

اَلَمْ تَرَ   اَلَمْ اَقُلْ   عَنْهُمْ وَرَضُوْا

Tick the boxes when you know how to do them:
I know how to do *Ikhfaa meem saakin*   ☐
I know how to do *Izhaar meem saakin*   ☐

Activity 2.7

1. Have a look in the Holy Qur'aan and find at least five examples of *Ikhfaa meem saakin.* Explain why. (10 mins)

2. Have a look in the Holy Qur'aan and find at least five examples of *Izhaar meem saakin.* Explain why. (10 mins)

PART 3: THE RULES OF *MADD*
Lesson 30 *Madd* Part 1 (Prolonging the Sound)

Remember the **Letters of *Madd* (*huroofe Madd*)** are:
1. *Alif* which has a *zabar (fathah)* before it

قَالَ

2. *Wow saakin* which has a *pesh (dhammah)* before it

جُوْعٍ

3. *Yaa saakin* which has *zer (kasrah)* before it

حِيْنَ

There are two types of *Madd*:
Madde Aslee and *Madde Far-ee*.

Madde Aslee is when there is no *sukoon*, no *hamzah*, and no *tashdeed* after the Letters of *Madd*. Stretch the sound for 1 *Alif*.

حِيْنَ   جُوْعٍ   قَالَ

Note: 1 *Alif* can be measured by opening a closed finger or closing an opened finger.
I know how to do *Madde Aslee* ☐

Activity 3.1

1. Have a look in the Holy Qur'aan and find at least five examples of *Madde Aslee.* Explain why.
(10 mins)

Lesson 31 *Madd* (Part 2)

Madde Far-ee has four types:
Madde Muttasil, Munfasil, Laazim and *Aaridh*.

1. *Madde Muttasil*: If you see a *hamzah* after *harfe Madd* in a same word, stretch the sound for 2 to 6 *Alifs*.

السَّمَاءَ   شَاءَ   اُولَٰئِكَ

2. *Madde Munfasil*: If you see a *hamzah* after the *harfe Madd* in the next word, stretch the sound for 2 to 4 *Alifs*.

يَلْبَثُوْا اِلَّا   الَّذِيْ اَطْعَمَهُمْ   الَّذِيْ اَنْقَضَ   اِنَّا اَنْزَلْنٰهُ

3. *Madde Lazim*: If you see a *sukoon* after *harfe Madd* in the same word, stretch the sound for 3 to 5 *Alifs*.

آلْئٰنَ

4. *Madde Aaridh*: If after *harfe Madd* there is a *sukoon* because you stopped on that word, stretch the sound for 1 to 5 *Alifs*.

تَعْلَمُوْنَ   الرَّحْمٰنُ   الْعَظِيْمُ   اَخِيْهِ   سِجِّيْلٍ

Madde Leen: When you stop and there is a *zabar* before *wow saakin* or *yaa saakin*. Stretch the sound for 1 *Alif* (preferable) or 3 *Alifs*.

Tick the boxes once you know the rules:

I know how to do the four types of *Madde Far-ee* ☐

I know how to do *Madde Leen* ☐

Activity 3.2

1. Have a look in the Holy Qur'aan and find at least two examples of each *madd* from the four types. Explain why.
(15-20 mins)

2. Have a look in the Holy Qur'aan and find at least five examples of *Madde Leen*. Explain why.
(10 mins)

PART 4 THE RULES OF STOPPING AND CONTINUING RECITATION

Lesson 32 Rules of *Waqf* (Stopping)

When stopping at a word which has any one of these *harakaat* ◌َ ◌ِ ◌ُ on its last letter, then the last letter will be read with a *sukoon* ◌ْ . E.g.

When you stop at يَعْلَمُوْنَ you will read it as: يَعْلَمُوْنْ .

If the word you are stopping at has *do zabar* (*fathatain*) ◌ً on its last letter, then it will be read as an *Alif*. E.g.

When you stop at اَفْوَاجًا you will read it as: اَفْوَاجَا .

If the last letter is a round *taa* ة it will be read as a *haa* ه . E.g.

When you stop at جَنَّةٌ it will be read as جَنَّهْ .

If after *tanween* there is a *saakin* letter and you want to continue, then the *noon* of that *tanween* will be read with a *kasrah* and joined with the *saakin* letter. E.g.

When continuing then لُمَزَةٍ الَّذِىْ will be read as:
لُمَزَةِ نِ الَّذِىْ

If you decide to stop then the *noon* of *tanween* will not be read: لُمَزَةْ اَلَّذِىْ

Tick the boxes when you know the rules:

I know how to stop at *harakaat* ☐
I know how to stop at *do zabar* (*fathatain*) ☐
I know how to stop at round *taa* ☐
I have understood how to stop and continue where there is a *noon* of *tanween* ☐

Activity 4.1

1. Have a look in the Holy Qur'aan and find at least two *waqf* examples of the following:

(a) *Harakaat*
(b) *Do zabar (fathatain)*
(c) *Round taa*
(d) *Noon of tanween*

(10 mins)

Lesson 33 *Alif* and Stopping

اَنَا means 'I' in Arabic, and the *alif* at its end will never be read whilst continuing or stopping, so it will be read as *ana* not *anaa*.

Whenever there is a small circle above an *alif* اْ the *alif* will not be read when continuing. However, if you stop on the *alif* you must read it. For example: لٰكِنَّاْ هُوَ if continuing it will be read as لٰكِنَّ هُوَ and if you stop on it, the *alif* will be read as لٰكِنَّاْ هُوَ .

Tick the boxes when you know the rules:

I know how to read *ana* ☐
I know how to stop and continue when the *alif* has a small circle on top of it ☐

Lesson 34 Symbols of Continuing and Stopping in the Qur'an

ز *Mujawwiz*, continuing is better.

ق *Qaaf*, continuing is better.

صل *Sil*, continuing is better.

صلّى *al-Wasl*, continue.

ك *Kathaalik*, the rule is the same as the verse before it.

لا *Laa*, continue, do not stop here. This symbol is found in the middle of a verse.

لا۟ *Laa Waqf*, better to continue. This symbol is found at the end of a verse.

ﺹ *Waqfe Murakkhas*, better to continue. However, if the verse is long, then one can stop.

ﺝ *Waqfe Jaa-iz*, better to continue, to stop is also permissible.

ﻡ *Waqfe Laazim*, must stop.

ﻁ *Waqfe Mutlaq*, stop, do not join.

◯ *Aayah*, stop. The sentence has been completed.

ﻗﻒ *Qif*, stop.

ﺱ *Seen*, pause without taking a breath, then continue.

ﺳﻜﺘﺔ *Saktah*, pause without taking a breath, then continue.

وَقْفَة *Waqfah*, pause without taking a breath, but here the pause will be slightly longer than the previous two.

∴ This symbol is called مُعَانَقَة *Mu'aaniqah*, it will come twice wherever you see it. You will stop at one and continue on the other.

Tick the boxes when you know the symbols:

I know the symbols of continuing ☐
I know the symbols of stopping ☐

Activity 4.2

1. What do the following symbols mean:

(a) ڒ   (b) م   (c) لا   (d) ط

(e) ج   (f) سكتة   (g) ○

(15-20 mins)

Lesson 35 The Amount Symbols

الرّبع *ar-Rubu*, end of the first quarter of the *Juz* (*Para*).

النّصف *an-Nisf*, end of the first half of the *Juz*.

الثلثة *ath-Thalaathah*, end of the third quarter of the *Juz*.

ع
○ *Ruku*, a division according to meaning.

المنزل *al-Manzil*, the Holy Qur'an is divided into seven parts. A *Manzil* is one part of those seven parts.

Tick the boxes when you know the symbols:

I know the different symbols in the Holy Qur'an ☐

Lesson 36 The *Sajdah* of Recitation (*Tilaawat*)

The Beloved Messenger of Allah (peace be upon him) said: 'If a son of Adam recites an *ayat* of *sajdah* and does *sajdah*, Satan departs from him and cries: Alas! He was ordered to do *sajdah* and he did, so for him is Paradise. I was ordered to do *sajdah* and I disobeyed, so for me is Hell.' (Muslim and Ibn Majah)

There are 14 *sajdah* verses in the Holy Qur'an. Whenever one of the *sajdah ayats* is read or heard (even if the listener did not intend to hear it), it is *wajib* (obligatory) to do the *sajdah* of recitation (*tilawat*). The *sajdah* is not *wajib* if you heard the verse from a CD, tape or TV etc.

The *sajdah* of recitation has the same preconditions as *namaz*, and is *wajib* on those on whom *namaz* is *fardh* (obligatory), so it wouldn't be *wajib* for a child to perform or a woman in a state of *hayd* (menstruation) or *nifas* (post-natal bleeding).

If one recites the same *sajdah ayat* numerous times without moving from his place, he must only do one *sajdah*. If a person recites two different *sajdah ayats* in the same place, then he must do two *sajdahs* and so on. This same rule also applies to hearing the *sajdah ayats.*

How to do the Sajdah of recitation:
When you hear the *sajdah ayat,* say the t*akbeer,* then go into *sajdah* like you would for *namaz.* Say the *takbeer* again and rise from the *sajdah.*

The 14 sajdah ayats:

1. al-'Alaq verse 19
2. al-Inshiqaaq verse 21
3. al-Najm verse 62
4. Ha Meem verse 37
5. Saad verse 24
6. al-Sajdah 15
7. al-Naml verse 25
8. al-Furqaan verse 60
9. al-Hajj verse 18
10. Maryam 58
11. al-Isra verse 107
12 al-Nahl verse 49
13. al-Ra'd verse 15
14. al-A'raaf verse 206

I know the rules of the *sajdah tilawat* ☐
I know where to find the *sajdah ayats* ☐

My Personal Advice and Tips for Teachers

These are rules which I have developed in a madrasah classroom setting when teaching children aged between 7 and 12. They really helped create an environment where the students were learning and improving their Tajweed with great results *alhamdulillah*. You can apply the rules which you think will be helpful in your setting.

When you are reading to the students and they read after you:

a) Emphasise whatever the student reads incorrectly through showing and not telling. For example, the student missed out an *alif* in a verse you just read to him, you need to read that verse again but this time emphasise the *alif* more than the rest of the words. On the rare occasion, the student does not pick up on his mistake, you then need to explain to him that he is missing out the *alif*.

b) I have a stopping and starting rule which I tell my students: Stop exactly where I stop, start exactly where I start from. Generally, I ask them to start from the closest *wa*, *fa*, *thumma* or *illaa*. This helps their recitation have more fluency and avoids changing the meaning of the Holy Qur'an. Stopping at every three words is for beginners and as they progress they should be gently nudged to stop only when they need to, rather than forcing themselves to stop after three words.

c) Another rule I tell my students, is: Copy the way I pronounce the letters. For example, if I say *'ayn*, you should make an *'ayn* sound not a *hamzah* sound (which is a common mistake). If I say *qaaf*, you should say *qaaf* not *kaaf*. And so on. This does seem obvious, but many students forget this rule. So from time to time it must be repeated.

d) I ask the students to listen and follow the recitation with their index finger whether I am reading to them or whether their classmate is reading to me. This rule applies to all the students, even if they made no mistakes that day when they read to me.

e) I ask them to underline any new words or difficult words, and to make sure they don't make a mistake on those words. I also tell them the common mistakes made in the difficult/new words and notice that they never make those mistakes.

f) I always remind my students the need to recite every letter correctly by giving them the example of *qalb* and *kalb*. When we recite this word with a *qaaf* (as *qalb*), it means heart. When we recite this word with a *kaaf* (as *kalb*) it means dog. Just by changing one letter, the meaning has completely changed. So we need to pronounce every letter correctly, so that we don't change the meaning of the Holy Qur'an.

When the student reads to you:

a) If the student makes a mistake on a word or misses a rule of Tajweed out which was covered previously, then ask him/her questions about it rather than giving the answer straight away. This will help the student realise when and how to apply the rule for himself. If the student does not recall the rule or struggles to identify what he is reading wrong, give the answer to him and tell him to re-learn the Tajweed rule and you will ask him to explain it to you first thing tomorrow.

b) I tell my students: when you read to me it must be your best recitation. You can't read in front of me like you're trying to work out the words, it must be better than that. This can be achieved easily by practicing what needs to be learnt, the more you practice, the less hesitation and trying to work out the words in front of the teacher.

c) I remind them my rule about same mistakes: You should hate same mistakes the way I hate same mistakes. This rule is really helpful to students as it gives them that extra boost to make sure they don't make same mistakes and as a result improves their recitation.

d) I have an underlining rule, which is that whenever a student makes a mistake in front of me they must underline their mistake with a blue pen. This helps the students during revision time as they know which words they need to spend more time on.

e) I remind my students to read the last letter of words which they stop on. For example, when stopping on *qadr*, *khusr*, *'asr*, *sabr*, to read the last letter *raw*. Also when *hamzah* is the last letter of the word you stop on, to make sure the sound of *hamzah* is made in *shaa*. Lastly, pray for your students and ask Allah to help them in their learning, increase their knowledge and practice of Islam. This will increase empathy and good character in the teacher which is very much needed in our times.

Bibliography

Ibn al-Jazari, *Al-Muqaddimah al-Jazariyyah*, Qadimi Kutub Khana, Karachi, Pakistan.

(Imam Ibn al-Jazari (1350-1429) is regarded as an authority in Qur'anic recitation. He wrote the famous poem on Tajweed called the *Muqaddimah* which is considered a classic and taught all over the world. I was taught the *Muqaddimah* at the Institute of Islamic Education and found his poem helpful in learning Tajweed, and so I used it as the main source for my book as well as tips given to me by my teachers).

© 2016 Khalid Idris
ISBN: 978-1-326-74623-0

Printed in Great Britain
by Amazon